THE
MARCH ON
WASHINGTON

SAMUEL WILLARD CROMPTON

Rosen
YA™
New York

Published in 2018 by The Rosen Publishing Group, Inc.
29 East 21st Street, New York, NY 10010

Copyright © 2018 by The Rosen Publishing Group, Inc.

First Edition

Library of Congress Cataloging-in-Publication Data

Names: Crompton, Samuel Willard, author.
Title: The March on Washington / Samuel Willard Crompton.
Description: New York : Rosen Publishing, 2018. | Series: Spotlight on the civil rights movement | Includes bibliographical references and index. | Audience: Grades 5–10.
Identifiers: LCCN 2017019729| ISBN 9781538380529 (library bound) | ISBN 9781538380499 (pbk.) | ISBN 9781538380505 (6 pack)
Subjects: LCSH: March on Washington for Jobs and Freedom (1963 : Washington, D.C.)—Juvenile literature. | Civil rights demonstrations—Washington (D.C.)—History—20th century—Juvenile literature. | African Americans—Civil rights—History—20th century—Juvenile literature.
Classification: LCC F200 .C76 2017 | DDC 323.1196/073009046—dc23
LC record available at https://lccn.loc.gov/2017019729

Manufactured in China

On the cover: Crowds thronged the Mall in Washington, DC, for one of the most best-known events of the civil rights movement, the March on Washington for Jobs and Freedom.

CONTENTS

THE BIGGEST MARCH 4

THE NEED 6

THE GRAND OLD MAN .8

THE 1963 MARCH 10

JFK 12

EARLY MORNING 14

THE CROWDS ARRIVE 16

THE SHORT MARCH 18

THE SINGERS 20

THE FIRST SPEAKERS 22

THE FLAMETHROWER 24

THE PREACHER 26

BUILDING THE SPIRIT 28

"I HAVE A DREAM" 30

MEETING THE PRESIDENT 32

THE REACTION 34

ASSASSINATION 36

THE CIVIL RIGHTS ACT 38

LEGACY OF THE MARCH ON WASHINGTON 40

GLOSSARY 42

FOR MORE INFORMATION 43

FOR FURTHER READING 45

BIBLIOGRAPHY 46

INDEX 47

THE BIGGEST MARCH

On August 28, 1963, roughly 250,000 people converged on the Mall in Washington, DC. They were black and white, rich and poor. Many of them had suffered racial discrimination, although some had not.

The marchers came from all parts of the United States. Most came from states in the East, Midwest, and South. Rather few West Coast Americans made it to the march, but many were there in spirit. The marchers came by bus, automobile, and train, and a few arrived by airplane. Surely the most unusual of all the marchers, however, was Ledger Smith. The twenty-seven-year-old African American roller-skated from downtown Chicago. He made it to Washington, DC, in ten short days.

Ledger's appearance was the most dramatic. His heroic means of transport stood for the efforts of thousands of others, however. Many people sacrificed to participate in the march.

More than two hundred thousand people came to the elegant but crowded space at the Mall on August 28, 1963. The Washington Monument is in the background.

THE NEED

In the winter of 1963, the civil rights movement appeared stalled. Significant gains had been made in the previous eight years, but millions of African Americans were still treated like second-class citizens in their own country. Segregation and other abuses persisted in the South.

In 1955, a group of African American leaders made a major move by boycotting the segregated public buses in Montgomery, Alabama. The boycott lasted slightly longer than a year, and it ended in complete victory for the protestors—the Supreme Court ruled that making African Americans sit in the back of the bus was unconstitutional. The success encouraged African Americans, and many white admirers, to fight more strongly for civil rights.

The very success in Montgomery led to stronger resistance, however. Alabama witnessed some of the nastiest examples of

A Tallahassee, Florida, city bus is jeered at by African American students in 1956. The successful Montgomery bus boycott led to many similar protests.

white supremacy. African American protest marchers were often attacked, and some of them were beaten mercilessly.

In the spring of 1963, a handful of African American leaders announced the March on Washington for Jobs and Freedom. The title was created by the grand old man of protest movements.

THE GRAND OLD MAN

Born in Florida in 1889, Asa Philip Randolph was the oldest of all the African American protest leaders. Moving to New York City as a young man, he became an established businessman and a spokesman for the black community.

In 1941, Randolph was the founding president of the United Brotherhood of Sleeping Car Porters. This union of ten thousand men was made up almost entirely of blacks. Randolph announced he would lead a protest march on Washington against the discrimination of black Americans in the US defense industry. Randolph rightly suspected that America would soon enter World War II. He wanted black workers to work in factories and plants that made tanks and planes.

The 1941 march did not happen. President Franklin D. Roosevelt signed an executive order prohibiting discrimination in defense industries. But Randolph had shown the potential power of the African American community.

Now, in 1963, he and other black leaders were ready to follow up on that potential to challenge segregation and poor job prospects.

Asa Philip Randolph was seventy-three years old in 1963. He was the grand old man of the march, while Martin Luther King Jr. was the shining young star.

THE 1963 MARCH

I
n 1963, Asa Philip Randolph was seventy-three. His mind was just as keen as ever, though. Randolph lived in Manhattan, and he became the number one organizer for the 1963 March on Washington. The event would protest discrimination and show Congress that the civil rights laws before them should be passed. Randolph planned for the event to happen in late summer.

Randolph could not pull off the march by himself. He turned to religious leaders in the black community, as well as to younger people who had recently become protestors. As summer approached, it was apparent that Randolph and his coleaders, who were called the Big Six, were close to success.

The Brotherhood of Sleeping Car Porters celebrated its thirtieth anniversary in 1955. Led by Asa Philip Randolph, this was the first successful union composed largely of African American workers.

There was a major question mark, however. How would the US government respond to having Washington, DC, taken over, even if only for one day? The answer to this could only come from one man: the president of the United States.

JFK

Born in Boston in 1917, John F. Kennedy was now president of the United States. At forty-six, he was the youngest man ever elected to the White House.

Kennedy's nickname was JFK, for his initials. As a young, handsome, and idealistic president, JFK seemed well suited to help the civil rights movement. But leaders of the African American community, including Asa Randolph, were disappointed in JFK's slow movement on civil rights measures.

In the late summer of 1963, JFK was preoccupied. His wife, Jacqueline Bouvier Kennedy, was in the last stages of a pregnancy. On August 3, 1963, the First Lady gave birth to an underweight baby boy. He died two days later.

JFK's grief was a good reason for him not to be involved in the March on Washington. He did pledge to meet with the march's leaders, however.

John F. Kennedy was a very popular president. Skilled at public relations, he handled the Washington, DC, press corps with humor and charm.

EARLY MORNING

Randolph and his fellow organizers decided that the march would be held on August 28, 1963. They put the word out. And people came to Washington, DC, in buses, taxicabs, and trains. The first participants arrived at about 2:30 a.m.

These early comers found the city practically deserted. Many city residents went away for a few days, and most of the federal government employees did not go to work. This is because they knew there would be a tremendous crowd, tying up what was a crowded city on even the best of days.

The first-comers set up some tents. They prepared for what would be a much-larger crowd. But for the first five hours, an eerie quietness prevailed. Some marchers feared they had been overly optimistic about the number of people that would come. It still did not seem possible that a quarter of a million people were on their way.

The national headquarters of the march were in Harlem. The official title, shown on the banner, was the March on Washington for Jobs and Freedom

THE CROWDS ARRIVE

At 7:30 a.m. there were still more police than marchers. The District of Columbia had 5,900 men on hand, including 1,700 National Guardsmen. It seemed that the march might have been overadvertised, that it might not deliver. But at around 8:00 a.m. came the "Freedom Special," a train all the way from Jacksonville, Florida, carrying 785 marchers. Many of them had recently participated in protests in Alabama, and not a few of them wore scars as a result. From the moment these Southerners arrived, the tone of the march changed. It became more jubilant.

Thousands of other marchers arrived between 8:00 and 11:00 a.m. By 11:30, it was obvious that the march would deliver. The organizers had succeeded. Thanks to their efforts, the march would bring more protestors to one place than at any previous time in American history.

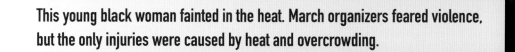

This young black woman fainted in the heat. March organizers feared violence, but the only injuries were caused by heat and overcrowding.

THE SHORT MARCH

Thousands of people—black and white, from far-off and nearby—had already made the long trip to Washington, DC. The final leg of their journey was the eight-tenths of a mile from the Washington Monument to the Lincoln Memorial. This, the "short march," was supposed to begin at 11:30. Some of the newest arrivals were overeager, however, and the short march began spontaneously at about 11:10.

Seeing the crowd's impatience, the Big Six began to lead the march. They were Asa Philip Randolph, John Lewis, Roy Wilkins, Whitney Young Jr., James Farmer, and the Reverend Martin Luther King Jr. With these men in front, the march took on a powerful appearance.

The march began twenty minutes early because of the gathering crowd pressure. Martin Luther King Jr. is in the center of the leaders of the march.

While the march began, millions of Americans watched from the comfort of their living rooms. As television sets beamed the images, many white Americans were impressed by the size of the crowd and its quiet spirit.

THE SINGERS

The March on Washington had a joyous, even light-hearted attitude thanks to the energy of the people who had come so far. It was also due to the music, produced by many popular and talented musicians.

Standing in the shadow of the Lincoln Memorial, the band Peter, Paul, and Mary played some of the favorite songs of the time. They were followed by Joan Baez and the young Bob Dylan. Dylan had recently become a hero of the world of folk music through the release of "Blowin' in the Wind," a song well-known among those who struggled for civil rights.

Professional actors also came to the stage. Charlton Heston was known as the leading star of several epic films based on the

Joan Baez and Bob Dylan were up-and-coming folk musicians who performed at the march. Both went on to have long-lasting careers.

Bible, such as *The Ten Commandments*. Marlon Brando came to the stage, where he held up an electric cattle prod. Everyone understood that cattle prods were sometimes used by southern police to intimidate African American protestors.

THE FIRST SPEAKERS

Asa Philip Randolph gave the first speech. Sadly, the grand old organizer was not a fine speechmaker. Oratory had never been his strong point. But those who listened took away a powerful feeling. Randolph gave his blessing to the March of 1963, while reminding the marchers that something similar had almost happened in 1941.

Walter Reuther was leader of the UAW, the United Auto Workers of America. He was the only white person to take the podium that day. Reuther gave a fine speech about the labor movement, the civil rights movement, and the common goals they shared. The crowd liked what Reuther had to say.

The leaders and organizers of the march gathered at the Lincoln Memorial in the shadow of the sixteenth American president, who had emancipated the slaves a century earlier.

By now there were at least two hundred thousand people in and around the Mall. It seemed as if the crowd might become too large to keep order. But though the police and National Guard looked on, they found no significant disturbances.

THE FLAMETHROWER

John Lewis was the fourth person to give a speech. Only twenty-three years old, Lewis was a rising star in the civil rights movement. He had been badly beaten by white supremacists in Alabama two years earlier when participating in the Freedom Rides, a bus convoy that protested segregation in transportation.

Lewis gave a fiery speech. He demanded Congress approve President Kennedy's recent proposed legislation. The crowd applauded Lewis, but they did not know he had written an even tougher speech. The Catholic archbishop of Washington had seen an early version of that speech and demanded it be toned down. As a result, Lewis came across as tough, even aggressive, but not out of control.

After John Lewis came Mahalia Jackson, a much-admired singer of the time. Jackson sang "I've Been Buked and I've Been Scorned." Many, if not most, people in the crowd were deeply moved.

Mahalia Jackson was a talented African American singer. She sang "I've Been Buked and I've Been Scorned" minutes before Martin Luther King Jr. came to the podium.

THE PREACHER

The Reverend Martin Luther King Jr. came to the podium. He needed no introduction.

Born in Atlanta in 1929, King was only thirty-four, but he looked and acted much older. King had a serious demeanor, and the cut of his clothes—dark, tailor-made suits—made him seem quite conservative. In a social sense, King was conservative. He believed in the power of family, faith, and male leadership. In terms of race relations, he was a revolutionary, a person who believed in full integration between whites and blacks. His practice of leading nonviolent protests made him the most recognizable figure of the civil rights movement.

Arriving at the podium, King began with serious but also quiet words. "The Negro," he declared, "lives in a lonely island of poverty in the midst of a vast ocean of material prosperity."

As he approached the podium, Martin Luther King Jr. was the best-known African American leader. Eight years earlier, he had organized the Montgomery bus boycott.

Almost everyone in the crowd agreed. Most of them toiled at jobs, working long hours for low pay. But they were concerned with more than material means. They wanted to hear about the moral tone of America.

BUILDING THE SPIRIT

In the middle of his speech, Reverend Martin Luther King Jr.'s voice rose. He spoke with passion about the condition of black people in the land their hands had done so much to build.

"This sweltering summer of the Negro's legitimate discontent will not pass," King declared. He wanted the nation to move, rapidly, in the direction of social and economic equality. Many people in the immediate audience had heard these words before. But for many that watched on television, this was the first time.

When King spoke about the summer of discontent, the crowd came fully into his hand. They shouted "Yes, yes!" to

"I Have a Dream" was the greatest speech of King's career. In a few minutes, he transformed the feelings of thousands of people in person and millions who watched on TV.

almost every sentence he said. And King saved his best for last. It was in the final two minutes that he moved to his words about a dream, a dream of a new America that would long outlive the man himself.

"I HAVE A DREAM"

"I have a dream! I have a dream that one day on the red hills of Georgia the sons of former slaves and the sons of former slave-owners will be able to sit down together at the table of brotherhood." These words won tremendous applause, but King was not finished.

The son and grandson of Baptist ministers, King may not have known it, but he had prepared most of his life for this very moment. Nearly a quarter of a million people listened, wept, and chanted as he moved to his conclusion.

King evoked images of the worst types of white racism. He spoke of Stone Mountain, in his native Georgia, a place that saw

A skilled orator, King knew when to pause and when to let his speechmaking soar.

the rebirth of the Ku Klux Klan in 1915. But he concluded with hope, shouting that the children and grandchildren of slaves would one day be "free at last!"

MEETING THE PRESIDENT

Martin Luther King Jr.'s speech was the high point of the March on Washington. Though a few other people took the podium to make speeches, the main event had come and gone. Realizing this, the crowd began to fade.

The Big Six, as the march leaders were called, left the Mall and went to the White House. There they met with President John F. Kennedy and Vice President Lyndon B. Johnson. The photograph taken there shows President Kennedy near the middle of the group but Asa Philip Randolph at the precise center. Perhaps the photographer wanted to draw attention to Randolph's efforts. Perhaps JFK wanted the black organizer to

Leaders of the march met President Kennedy at the White House. The president was his usual self, charming but noncommittal where racial issues were concerned.

be at the center. In either case, the photograph showcased the black leaders.

JFK and Vice President Johnson did not do much for the march and its leaders, however. They congratulated the Big Six but made no promises about laws or regulations to come.

THE REACTION

Americans were stunned and amazed. Millions of them had expected the worst, fearing that the march would turn into a bloody riot. They were mistaken.

Millions of other Americans hoped and prayed that the march would make a profound difference in national policy. They hoped JFK and Congress would make giant strides toward equality by turning their attention to urgent civil rights abuses. They, too, were mistaken.

The journalists of *Time* magazine observed the march with great interest. One week after the event, they wrote their opinion that it had been a great success but that no one knew what would come after. *Time* quoted that the crowd shouted for freedom, and freedom now. "But 'Now!' remained a long way off. It would not come today, tomorrow, next month or next year."

The editors of *Time* magazine were often correct. But on this occasion they were wrong. Change would indeed come, and it would arrive in slightly less than a year.

A young girl stands in the crowd of the March on Washington for Jobs and Freedom, a reminder that it attracted all ages.

ASSASSINATION

Many Americans feared that the March on Washington would lead to increased violence. And there was an increase in some southern communities. But the major bloodshed that many people feared did not happen. Instead, there was one great loss, and it came at the highest level.

On November 22, 1963, less than three months after the march, President Kennedy was shot and killed in Dallas, Texas. There was no direct connection between the march and the president's assassination. Rather, JFK was killed by a lone gunman, acting on his own.

The president's death traumatized the nation. Black and white, rich and poor, Americans mourned the death of the handsome young leader who had shown such promise. African Amer-

Two African American women mourn outside the Parkland Hospital in Dallas, Texas. President Kennedy had just been assassinated.

icans grieved deeply. Though JFK had not been a major leader for civil rights, they still hoped he would come around. They had much less hope in Vice President Lyndon B. Johnson, the new president.

THE CIVIL RIGHTS ACT

Throughout the civil rights movement, people of all races were frequently surprised. One such surprise concerned the Civil Rights Act of 1964.

President John Kennedy was dead and in the grave. Vice President Lyndon B. Johnson—also known as LBJ—had become the thirty-sixth president of the United States.

In the spring of 1964, LBJ used all his political muscle to advocate for civil rights. He had previously been the majority whip in the US House of Representatives, so he knew his way around government. LBJ persuaded Congress to pass the Civil Rights Act of 1964. The act granted great power to the federal government to outlaw discrimination based on race, color, religion, sex, or national origin. It also ended segregation in public places. African Americans had been pushing for just such a law for a long time.

LBJ signed the Civil Rights Act into law on July 2, 1964.

When he became president, Lyndon B. Johnson was distrusted by many civil rights movement leaders, but he became a hero when he signed the Civil Rights Act of 1964.

LEGACY OF THE MARCH ON WASHINGTON

Virtually everyone who studies American history agrees that the march was one of the most important events of the twentieth century. It was the largest public gathering of the century to that date. Just as important, the march brought together people from every social and economic condition.

But how much did the march accomplish in the immediate aftermath? The answer is that the march could not solve all problems. It could not sweep away three centuries of bad feelings between blacks and whites. But the march did succeed

This granite plaque, on the steps of the Lincoln Memorial, honors Martin Luther King Jr. and the march.

on more than one level. It, and the subsequent assassination of JFK, persuaded the federal government to enact the Civil Rights Act of 1964. The march also set a new standard for popular protest. For the rest of the century, and well into the twenty-first century, the March on Washington was the standard for successful, nonviolent protest.

boycott The decision to reject use of a thing, commodity, or service.

discrimination The practice of treating people differently because of their age, race, gender, sexuality, or other factor out of their control.

editor Someone who directs the publication of a magazine, newspaper, or book.

folk music A musical style that developed in the early twentieth century and peaked in the 1960s.

integration To stop the separation of blacks and whites in American society, which was the goal of most of the civil rights protests.

journalist A person who reports the news.

labor movement A collection of groups, or labor unions, that worked to gain fair wages and working conditions for employees.

legislation Bills, in Congress or state legislatures, that can be turned into laws.

Lincoln Memorial The white marble memorial to President Abraham Lincoln in Washington, DC.

National Mall A national park located in Washington, DC.

oratory The art of speech-making.

podium A piece of furniture from which speeches are delivered.

segregation Strict separation of the races, which was enforced by law until the year 1954.

sleeping car The sections of a railroad train devoted to rest and comfort for the passengers.

union An official organization that represents the interests of employed people.

white supremacy The belief that whites are superior to blacks.

Canadian Centre for Diversity and Inclusion
2 Carlton Street, Suite 820
Toronto, ON M5B 1J3
Canada
(416) 968-6520
Website: http://ccdi.ca/
Facebook: @CCDISOCIAL
Twitter :@CCDITweets
Instagram: @ccdigrams
The centre provides experts in diversity, human rights, and equity
    within the workplace.

The King Center
449 Auburn Avenue NE
Atlanta, GA 30312
(404) 526-8900
Website: http://www.thekingcenter.org
Facebook: @thekingcenter
Twitter: @TheKingCenter
Dedicated both to the Reverend Martin Luther King Jr. and the con-
    tinuation of his work.

Lincoln Memorial
National Parks Service
900 Ohio Drive SW
Washington, DC 20024
(202) 426-6841
Website: https://www.nps.gov/linc/index.htm
Facebook: @nationalparkservice

Twitter: @natlparksservice

Instagram: @nationalparkservice

A monument in honor of the nation's sixteenth president, who served during the Civil War and endorsed the Thirteenth Amendment to the Constitution, which outlawed slavery.

National Civil Rights Museum, at the Lorraine Motel

450 Mulberry Street

Memphis, TN 38103

(901) 521-9699

Website: https://www.civilrightsmuseum.org

Facebook: @NCRMuseum

Twitter: @NCRMuseum

Instagram: @ncrmuseum

This museum is set at the site where Martin Luther King Jr. was assassinated. It focuses on the history of the civil rights movement.

WEBSITES

Because of the changing nature of internet links, Rosen Publishing has developed an online list of websites related to the subject of this book. This site is updated regularly. Please use this link to access this list:

http://www.rosenlinks.com/SCRM/March

Chorlian, Meg. *March on Washington*. Peterborough, NH: Cobblestone Publishing, 2013.

Jeffrey, Gary. *Martin Luther King Jr. and the March on Washington*. New York, NY: Gareth Stevens, 2013.

Johnson, Robin. *March on Washington*. New York, NY: Crabtree Publishing, 2013.

Krull, Kathleen. *What Was the March on Washington?* New York, NY: Grosset and Dunlap, 2013.

Lewis, John. *March. Book Two*. Marietta, GA: Top Shelf Productions, 2015.

Lewis, J. Patrick. *Voices from the March on Washington: Poems*. Honesdale, PA: Wordsong, 2014.

Tisdale, Rachel. *The March on Washington*. New York, NY: PowerKids Press, 2014.

Watson, Stephanie. *Martin Luther King Jr. and the March on Washington*. Minneapolis, MN: Abdo, 2016.

Barber, Lucy G. *Marching on Washington: The Forging of an American Political Tradition.* Berkeley, CA: University of CA Press, 2002.

Bass, Patrick Henry. *Like A Mighty Stream: The March on Washington, August 28, 1963.* Philadelphia, PA: Running Press, 2002.

Euchner, Charles C. *Nobody Turn Me Around: A People's History of the 1963 March on Washington.* Boston, MA: Bacon Press, 2010.

Gentile, Thomas. *March on Washington: August 28, 1963.* Washington, DC: New Day Publications, 1983.

Hansen, Drew D. *The Dream: Martin Luther King Jr. and the Speech That Inspired a Nation.* New York, NY: Ecco, 2003.

Kelley, Kitty. *Let Freedom Ring: Stanley Tretick's Iconic Images of the March on Washington.* New York, NY: Thomas Dunne Books, 2013.

Time. "*Civil Rights: The March's Meaning.*" September 6, 1963. http://content.time.com/time/magazine/article/0,9171,870445,00.html.

Williams, Juan. *Eyes on the Prize: America's Civil Rights Years, 1954–1965.* New York, NY: Viking, 1987.

B

Baez, Joan, 20
Big Six, 10, 32
Brando, Marlon, 21

C

Civil Rights Act of 1964, 38, 41
civil rights movement, 6, 12, 22, 26, 38

D

Dylan, Bob, 20

F

Farmer, James, 18
Freedom Rides, 24
"Freedom Special" train, 16

H

Heston, Charlton, 20–21

I

"I Have a Dream" (King), 30–31

J

Jackson, Mahalia, 24
jobs, and civil rights movement, 8, 9, 27
Johnson, Lyndon B., 32–33, 38

K

Kennedy, John F., 12, 32–34, 36–37
King, Martin Luther, Jr., 18, 26–32

L

labor movement, 8, 22
Lewis, John, 18, 24
Lincoln Memorial, 18

M

March on Washington for Jobs and
    Freedom
    attendance, 16, 23
    leaders of, 10, 32
    planning, 10–11
    singers and performers, 20–21, 24
    speakers, 22–24, 26–31
Montgomery bus boycott, 6–7

N

National Guard, 16, 23
nonviolent protest, 26, 41

P

Peter, Paul, and Mary, 20

R

Randolph, Asa Philip, 8–10, 12, 18, 22,
    32–33
Reuther, Walter, 22
Roosevelt, Franklin D., 8–9

S

segregation, 6, 9, 24, 38
Short March, the, 18–19
Smith, Ledger, 4
"summer of discontent," 28–29
Supreme Court ruling on segregation, 6

V

violence against protesters, 7, 16, 21

W

Wilkins, Roy, 18

Y

Young, Whitney, Jr., 18

ABOUT THE AUTHOR

Samuel Willard Crompton is the author of many books for young readers. He teaches history at Holyoke Community College, where he has seen the composition of the student body change greatly over the last twenty years. Crompton is a contributor to *Who's Who in African American History* and to the twenty-four-volume *American National Biography*. He has also appeared on TV as a commentator for the program *First Command* on the Military Channel.

PHOTO CREDITS